What We Missed

What We Missed

New and Selected Poems
in English, German, and French

Karen J. Head

Sandra Danneil, Editor
Randi Gunzenhäuser, Lead German Translator
Anne-Françoise Le Lostec, French Translator

Iris Press
Oak Ridge, Tennessee

Copyright © 2024 by Karen Head

All rights reserved. No portion of this book may be reproduced in any form or by any means, including electronic storage and retrieval systems, without explicit, prior written permission of the publisher, except for brief passages excerpted for review and critical purposes.

Cover Photograph: "Schiphol Airport, 2023"
by Colin Potts

Book Design: Robert B. Cumming, Jr.

Iris Press
www.irisbooks.com

*This book is dedicated
to the TU-Dortmund American Studies students
and teachers who, over twenty years,
formed the community that made this book possible.*

Contents

Introduction: A Place for Translation
Julia Sattler • 10

The Safe Space: A Students' Perspective
Lisa Schnickmann, Anna Krücken, and Emily Rose Weidle • 15

Looking Back: A Teacher's Perspective
Sandra Danneil • 16

Something Strange: A Poet's Perspective
Karen Head • 18

Do your best and apologize later: A Translator's Perspective
Anne-Françoise Le Lostec • 20

from *Shadow Boxes*

Legacy • 23
Vermächtnis • 23
Héritage • 24

Shadow Boxes • 25
Schaukästen • 25
Boîtes à souvenirs • 26

from *Sassing*

Hester Speaks • 28
Hester spricht • 30
Ainsi parle Hester • 32

Part of the Bargain • 34
Der Preis • 35
Un marché de dupes • 36

Emma's Tattoo • 37
Emmas Tattoo • 38
La tatouage d'Emma • 39

Instructions for my Burial Clothes • 41
Anweisungen für meinen Abgesang • 41
Consignes sur le choix de ma tenue funéraire • 42

from *My Paris Year*

My Paris Year Trois • 44
Mein Jahr in Paris Trois • 45
Mon Paris – Trois • 46

Day Trip:
My friend Randi suggests a New Post • 47
Tagesausflug:
Meine Freundin Randi schlägt mir einen neuen Posten vor • 47
Excursion d'un jour:
Mon amie Randi me suggère un nouveau poste • 48

from *On Occasion: Four Poets, One Year*

Guilty: A Valentine • 50
Schuldig: Ein Valentinsgedicht • 50
Preuve à charge: un billet de la Saint-Valentin • 51

May Day • 52
Erster Mai • 52
Jour de Mai • 53

Cleaning out the Pantry • 54
Vorräte aussortieren • 55
En rangeant le garde-manger • 56

from *Lost on Purpose*

Living in an old Flower Shop • 57
In einem alten Blumenladen wohnen • 57
Vivre dans une ancienne boutique de fleuriste • 58

At the Albion Beatnik Bookstore • 59
Im Albion Beatnik Buchladen • 60
Une visite à l'Albion Beatnik • 61

Lost on Purpose • 62
Mit Absicht verloren • 62
Égarées à dessein • 63

To the Roses of Auvillar • 65
An die Rosen von Auvillar • 66
Ode aux roses d'Auvillar • 67

Flight • 68
Im Flug • 68
Envol • 69

What we missed • 70
Was uns entging • 70
Les années que nous n'avons pas eues • 71

In my Kitchen in Atlanta • 72
In meiner Küche in Atlanta • 73
Dans ma cuisine à Atlanta • 74

Previously Uncollected Poems

Blues Harbor • 75
Blues Harbor • 77
Blues Harbor • 79

Olympia • 82
Olympia • 82
Olympie • 83

Perspective • 84
Perspektive • 85
Perspective • 87

The Dortmund Translation Group
Übersetzer:innengruppe
Technische Universität Dortmund

Paula-Sophie Brink
Sandra Danneil
Anna-Lena Drom
Johanna Feier
Hannah Folger
Pauline Fröhlich
Kim-Kristin Gaß
Jil Lara Gemmecke
Giulia Graw
Randi Gunzenhäuser
Lilian-Elisa Hachenberg
Igor Hoffmann
Kevin Lee Hüttenmüller
Jane Kaiser
Melda Kavak
Jannik Anton Klein
Laura Kost
Anna Krücken
Iris-Aya Laemmerhirt

Klara Sophia Lahme
Willem Petrus Leonardus Laschet
Lea Liebscher
Moana Zoe Elisabeth Mexner
Hanna Kristin Moukabary
Nadine Nett
Belma Pintol
Jan Ponert
Alina Brinza Pristescu
Thea Ressemann
Julia Sattler
Louisa Schlenger
Lisa Maria Schnickmann
Theresa Schwarz
Lea Spatzier
Alina Starostin
Emily Rose Weidle
Viktoria Maria Wenzel

Introduction: A Space for Translation

Julia Sattler

Throughout the past two decades, TU Dortmund University's American Studies Program has instituted what can be described as an English-to-German poetry-translation classroom of its own kind. In this classroom, translation becomes the primary mode of engaging with a text, and more specifically, with a poem or a collection of poems. Thus, the poem is interpreted via its translation.

Translation enables as well as necessitates the detailed analysis of the primary material, and, in the case of poetry, strengthens the reader's sensitivity to recognize stylistic devices and their effects. At the same time, as readers-as-translators they have to work on their expression in a different language, namely German – a language that is often their mother tongue. In the Dortmund poetry translation classroom, students and instructors work together and cooperate with each other in different formats. Dealing with poetry in a group is in some ways more akin to creative writing rather than to classical, i.e. individual approaches to translation. As a result, in the polyvocal translation singular voices can no longer be recognized – they have merged into one. Translation becomes a collective effort and community product.

Over the years, several well-received publications have come out of this rather unique setting for poetry translation: the translation of the poetry of former US President Jimmy Carter, the translation of June Jordan's 1997 *Kissing God Goodbye* into German, and the first German translation of Walt Whitman's 1855 version of *Leaves of Grass*. Currently, Dortmund students and instructors are engaging with the translation of the collection *Gravity* (1998) by the Second-Generation Holocaust author Elizabeth Rosner into German. The work of this poetry translation classroom has led to students at Dortmund becoming more interested in and open to poetry as a genre and in its potential in teaching. Several Bachelor and Master theses written in this setting also deal with translation: be it in the form of comparing different translations of the same text or in the form of engaging in translating a text yet unpublished in German.

When the Covid-19 pandemic made in-classroom meetings impossible in the spring semester of 2020, a group of instructors in Dortmund's American Studies Program decided to do a digital translation classroom engaging with the poetry of Karen Head. Karen Head, currently Associate Provost for Faculty Affairs at Augusta University in Georgia, has been a friend and affiliate of the TU Dortmund University for about 20 years. Karen Head's annual visit to the department is a defining moment of every fall semester; a time in which she not only offers precious advice to Dortmund instructors, but also offers lectures and practice sessions on academic writing and presentations.

Over the years, students became increasingly aware of Karen Head as a poet and thus asked for poetry readings during her visits. From this emerged the idea to engage with her poems via translating them into German. While this idea had existed for years, the digital classroom provided the opportunity of bringing together not only around 30 students and six Dortmund instructors, but also both Karen Head herself and her French translator, Anne-Françoise Le Lostec, a French-born instructor of German from Atlanta. The digital classroom quite literally created the space for group translation and reflection in the middle of the global pandemic.

Content and Form: On Techniques and Technologies

While poetry is often taught in the German American-Studies classroom, it is quite unusual to make space for its translation into German. Translation, if used in the education of future English teachers or other professionals, tends to be used in the context of teaching the foreign language's grammar and syntax. This kind of translation, usually from German into English, helps students understand structural markers of their own as well as of the foreign language. However, we think translation can and should be extended to converting texts from English into German: In Dortmund, we successfully engage with a poem in the word-for-word and line-by-line mode. This strategy often brings forward crucial questions about the workings of language and of poetry at large, but also about a specific text's layered meanings. This also concerns meanings that are not immediately evident when reading a poem, or analyzing it in relation to its formal features, themes, or registers.

In the Dortmund translation classroom, all students and instructors involved meet weekly for 90 minutes – the duration of a regular class session in a German university. But much of the work of the translation classroom actually takes place outside these one and a half hour sessions.

In addition to the regular class meetings that make space for discussion and questions, students meet and work in small groups of two or three with one instructor accompanying their translation process. In these small sessions, during which a poem is prepared for its detailed presentation in class, students tend to start from a rough word-for-word translation and then begin to negotiate with each other which translation, which term, which expression comes closest to their interpretation of the text. They will put together a first 'final' version of the translation to be made available to the other class participants and to be discussed in the session.

Each 90-minute class session starts from the original English-language text and its preliminary translation, which is then opened up for commentary by all participants – a process that can sometimes lead to the emergence of a new translation that is quite different from what it was at the start of the session. During the process of translating Karen Head's writing, the smaller group meetings, just like the larger ones, had to take place digitally. Despite the – certainly relevant – assumption that digital classrooms can contribute to social isolation, for many of the class's participants these meetings became an important part of their semester. The translation classroom was a space of encounter with just a small number of others to talk about something intimate like a poem and its translation, and thus differed majorly from listening to an online lecture, for example. Consequently, the process of translation quickly became one instance of staying connected in an otherwise isolating situation and explains why many students participated in the format not for one, but for two or even three semesters.

Often, the students' relationships with each other, but also their engagement with Karen Head's poetry went further than previously expected. For each session, the teams developed their own special presentation format – a video clip, a song, a slide show brimming with photographs of the settings and scenes the students had envisioned during their translation process. This demonstrates that the process of translation itself is inspiring and makes a poem more accessible to the students. The material provided by the groups then led to vivid discussion in the digital seminar room. Group members hailed from different study programs and different backgrounds, thus bringing in their own reading and their own strategies of dealing with the material provided. At times, we completely replaced the first interpretation, making sure its meanings still carried over. This was the moment where the translation became truly collective. Over three semesters, the book at hand was created from at least thirty different readings and revisions. Each line has been revised so many times that individual contributions can no longer be distinguished. The translations started to form a greater whole and this book came into being.

The process of collective translation was eased by two factors. The first was the presence of Karen Head as well as of Anne-Françoise Le Lostec in all major gatherings – an opportunity created by the pandemic. Despite the time difference between Germany and the USA this led to a much more intimate relationship between the poet and her translators than is usual in translation work. The digital classroom made space for vibrant intercultural dialogue.

The regular contributions by Karen and Anne-Françoise certainly made the translation process very different from other translation projects: Karen Head was there to answer questions relating to places and people mentioned throughout her work, but also to offer explanations concerning American popular culture and the US South, both crucial ingredients of her upbringing. Her French translator could speak about her own process of converting the poems from English into French. While actively dealing with three languages in the classroom, we came to realize that different language cultures brought with them comparable challenges that could mutually enlighten each other.

You as a reader can also compare the original text to its French and German versions in order to discover many different meanings in each poem. Especially idioms or metaphors tend to be very difficult to translate, as a word-for-word approach often does not make sense and an expression might be altogether unfamiliar in French, or German, or both. At times, it turned out that French and German were more alike than English and German, and the German translation then could learn from the French. Overall, the translation became much more nuanced as even more layers of meaning could be discovered by the translators through their ongoing dialogue with the writer and her French translator.

Before everything else, it was necessary to establish theoretical background knowledge about translating. Thus, we read Lawrence Venuti's "The Translator's Invisibility" (*Criticism* 28, 2. 1986: 179-212.) to critically reflect on our role as translators of Head's work. Recognizing that translation is an "active intervention of the translator" (182) and thus of a "profoundly transformative nature" (ibid.), students had to consider how 'visible' they wanted to be as co-authors of the translation. When translating, according to Venuti, there is always more than one possibility to state something, making a translation the outcome of a process of weighing different possibilities of phrasing and expressing something (184).

Poetry's innumerous stylistic devices from alliterations to language flow pose specific challenges to translation and can even make elaboration necessary to explore an expression in more detail. At times, this forced the group of translators to circumscribe something rather than state it directly, or ignore the fluency of a statement in the interest of keeping a pattern of alliterations in the text. In the present translation, the co-authors are indeed more visible at some points than at others – making evident that indeed "translation is the unstable reconciliation of two different, sometimes conflicting, sets of cultural determinations" (209). It is by no means a neutral process, and fraught with difficulty – how does one incorporate an author's specific register; how does one deal with local specificity that often cannot be translated? And yet, by the time our third class had reached its end, a more or less consistent translation of the work was available – not yet ready for publication, but refined to the point of a final process of editing.

Learning from Translation: A Conclusion

Incorporating translation – literary translation, poetry translation – into the American Studies curriculum enables students to become even more nuanced in their use of the foreign language, but also in their use of German. It sets in motion a process of carefully weighing multiple possibilities when expressing oneself, especially in written form. But it also helps students to fine-tune words to emotion and lose their fear of complex material such as poetry, oftentimes not their favorite genre when they begin their studies.

Approaching poetry via translation differs much from focusing only on form, or only on content, as is sometimes the case in school: Negotiating the complexities of translating a text, whether it be short or long, makes the students feel actively involved in the analysis, the interpretation, but also in the mediation. Poetry becomes alive via translation – it is no longer only the written word on the page, but it is something that can be expressed in different ways, that can be performed, and that can be passed on to others. Translation is certainly a strategy of reading poetry, but it is also so much more.

The Safe Space: A Students' Perspective

Lisa Schnickmann, Anna Krücken, and Emily Rose Weidle

We students had only little translation experience at the beginning of the project. We did not know what to expect, especially since it was part of the first semester that was taught online in early 2020.

The pandemic spread uncertainty in many areas of our academic and personal lives, but this project gave us a weekly meeting to look forward to. As the sessions were held online, we were afraid of not being able to connect with the other participants, the teachers, and especially Karen. However, Karen's open personality managed to break down the divide between teachers and students and helped unite us into a group of translators.

The weekly sessions and the warm atmosphere gave us a sense of stability in times of crisis. After we had overcome the initial organizational hurdles, the working atmosphere developed into a safe space. A safe space for creative processes, where each participant had a voice that was heard and appreciated. The deeper we delved into the poetic material, the more diverse the presentations became. Not only did we present our linguistic thoughts, but we also channeled our ideas into creative interpretations with visual illustrations, colorful collages, melancholic video sequences, and self-composed music.

While we were primarily concerned with getting the exact tone and atmosphere in the individual translations down on paper, we also managed to create a relaxed but disciplined working atmosphere within the group. On behalf of the students, we would like to thank everyone involved for this great opportunity. Not only did we learn something that will help us to be much more attentive to language in the future but above all, it is the time we spent together and the memories of exciting discussions that will stay in our minds.

Looking Back: A Teacher's Perspective

Sandra Danneil

I don't know where I'm going.
But, I sure know where I've been.
– David Coverdale

With this intro from the 1987 hit "Here I Go Again," David Coverdale, frontman of the British rock legend Whitesnake, sings his way into the heart of Karen Head. At this time, the young woman is in her early twenties and travels the world, surfing on a spirit of moving forward, keeping the eyes wide open for places she might later like to remember. She still doesn't know where she is going.

But later, as a poet, she surely knew where she had been when she kept alive the memories of her former life, of her grandparents' dogwood tree, Dolly Parton's clicking fingernails, encounters in a tiny French bookstore. And she wanted to let the world know about these people, places, and fantasies.

We encountered Karen's poetry during the Corona years, when life was limited to a minimum of interaction and a maximum of stagnation. Vistas linking the past to the present, let alone the future, became rare. In these trying times it was necessary to reclaim a larger perspective. It was hard to bridge the distance between places and people when, for example, in Germany people weren't allowed to even share a park bench with a friend. Our computers became our main window onto the world.

As the saying goes, when the eye gets blind, the soul takes over. During the pandemic, everybody searched for new forms of seeing. When students and teachers were longing for possible perspectives, Karen came to Dortmund via the World Wide Web and offered an insight into an earlier time, days of a past constructed in poetry. Karen took us on a poetic journey to places she had been to, invited us to her ways of seeing things in earlier stages of her life.

When we started the translation project, we had no idea where we were going or how long it would take us to get there - to translate a series of poems that offered a time travel into Karen's past life. For three semesters, a great number of students volunteered to translate and prepare, moderate and argue, perform and listen.

Every week students and teachers digged deeper into the words of a poet from the American South whose memories became our otherworldly fantasies of a long-forgotten past. Computer windows opened up to faces that showed relief as we gathered. Travelling back in time, our Wednesday meetings thus preserved the warming glow of early summer evenings, the sight of blood on a photograph, the sound of Blind Faith singing "Can't Find My Way Home" - a bumpy trip.

Karen's poetry inspired all of us to go beyond the word by word translation from one language into another. And so the weekly evenings became melancholic, for example when students presented their own musical compositions alongside Karen's lyrics, establishing a soundtrack for our joint venture, or funny when students created drawings and collages as the picture book of our shared emotions.

The soul took over its work like I have never seen it happen before or after in a university session. We didn't know where we were going. But we sure knew where we wanted to be during those Wednesday evenings.

Something Strange: The Poet's Perspective

Karen Head

For nearly twenty years, I have been a visiting scholar and artist at TU Dortmund. A couple of years into my annual visits, someone made a joke that I should be the poet laureate of Dortmund, and while it is unlikely the city would ever bestow such an honor on me, I did contemplate the idea long enough to write a poem about it.

During my visit in 2019, we began to discuss the idea of working on a translation of my poetry as part of a seminar in American studies. Arrangements were made and I was to spend the summer of 2020 in Dortmund helping to teach the seminar.

By late March of 2020, it was clear that the pandemic would prevent me from traveling, but a group of instructors and students still wanted to pursue the project. That initial term was followed by two successive terms – no one, it seemed, wanted the project to end. And, so, for months we met via videoconference.

In the second term of our project, my French translator, Anne-Françoise Le Lostec, began joining the seminar. She also has the benefit of being a fluent German speaker, so her extensive knowledge as a translator, along with her fluency in the three languages we were working with, made her a critically important member of our team.

It is a strange experience to be part of a translation project that takes as its topic your own work. Translation necessarily involves a keen sense of analysis, and it has been fascinating to discover things about my work I would never have noticed without this experience. It was also interesting to listen to the translators negotiate about the best possible word choices and diction, especially when the target language made translation difficult.

It was also interesting to watch as other translation challenges arose, especially those that were generational. Often, we had discussions between the instructors and the students that focused on how language changes over time, that is, how there were, in the students' minds, words and expressions that were outdated or had evolved to mean different things. There were also discussions about regional dialects and expressions. For my part, I learned not only more about my own poetry, but also about subtleties of German and French.

At times, the experience has felt mildly schizophrenic – with me needing to negotiate the often-contradictory roles of being the writer of the source text AND one of the translation instructors. Ultimately, I discovered that "Writer me" and "Reader me" could be different people. This was particularly evident when we found ourselves struggling with a translation element that was, essentially, untranslatable – when I would hear myself arguing to make the change that would most help the target language audience understand the "idea" of the poem rather than the actual image or reference I wrote.

Overall, I have been humbled and honored to work with this team. I am enormously grateful for the care they have taken with my work, and their desire to create meaningful and faithful translations. In the end, I believe this experience has made me a better writer.

Do your best and apologize later: A Translator's Perspective

Anne-Françoise Le Lostec

I'd like to begin by thanking Karen Head for sponsoring my work in this project, generously sharing some of her own funds and securing monetary assistance from the Ivan Allen College and my own department of Modern Languages at the Georgia Institute of Technology where I teach French and German. Most of all, Karen, thank you for your unwavering trust and friendship.

The invitation to join in an online Seminar led by Prof. Dr. Randi Gunzenhäuser and her wonderful team of young professors at the TU-Dortmund came right at the start of the pandemic and the weekly meetings with the students proved not only to be a thoroughly thought-provoking source of inspiration but also a lifeline in troubled times.

From the get-go, the sessions were a translator's dream: each team of students came ready to defend their work, each with their own brand of creativity and sensitivity. There were many eye-opening moments for me, listening to them arguing about their choices. Those moments can be tender when you've put your mind and hours of work into a translation! More than once, their insights made me go back to my own drawing board and reconsider my choices. I would like to thank them all for their very real contribution to my translations.

In-between meetings, I had my own moments of solitude, working on a French translation in a predominantly English-German endeavor. I am guilty of taking quite a few people hostage to my ruminations over the right word in numerous iterations of each poem. My first and most enduring victim being my dear husband, Richard. I also had a captive audience in my homebound parents in France and my sister Claire who always steers me true. I tested each poem in a version of the "gueuloir": reading the translation out loud to get a feel for the "perfect" version and because we all know that perfect doesn't exist in translation, we were chasing the most satisfying version instead.

When it comes to the most daring choices I made in this volume, I'd like to attract your attention to two poems where I took liberties with the original work: "Day Trip: My Friend Randi Suggests a New Post" and "Guilty: A Valentine." I'm pretty sure my fellow translators in the

Seminar would have had a lot to say about that but as Mary D. Hester Norton once famously said "a translator must do [her] very best – and then apologize for doing it at all."

Legacy

Shelling purple hulls and long white runners
I watched my grandfather rock under the dogwood tree.
Shining a buck-eye, he explained it would bring me luck.
More interested in his stories than his advice,
I was too young to realize they were one and the same.
His teeth gone for years and false ones on a shelf,
he could still eat corn on the cob and smile.
He learned to live without obstructions,
said things were simpler that way,
showed he loved me by offering a stick of Juicy-Fruit.
I popped it in my mouth,
the sweetness lingering a lifetime.

Vermächtnis

Beim Pellen von lila und weißen Stangenbohnen
beobachtete ich meinen Großvater im Schaukelstuhl unterm weißen
    Hartriegel.
Beim Polieren einer Kastanie erklärte er, sie würde mir Glück bringen.
Seine Geschichten interessierten mich mehr als seine Ratschläge;
ich war zu jung, um zu begreifen, dass sie ein und dasselbe waren.
Seit Jahren keine Zähne mehr, die Falschen im Schrank,
konnte er immer noch Maiskolben knabbern und lächeln.
Er hatte gelernt, ohne Einschränkungen zu leben,
sagte, alles wäre einfacher so,
zeigte, dass er mich liebte, mit einem Streifen Juicy-Fruit.
Ich stopfte ihn in den Mund,
süß ein Leben lang.

Héritage

Tout en décortiquant pois pourpres et haricots verts
je regardais mon grand-père sur son rocking chair se balancer sous le
    cornouiller.
Il lustrait un marron d'Inde, m'expliquant qu'il me porterait chance.
Plus intéressée par ses histoires que ses conseils,
je ne comprenais pas, dans mon jeune âge, qu'ils ne faisaient qu'un.
Édenté depuis des années, ses fausses dents remisées sur une étagère,
il pouvait encore manger son maïs sur l'épi et sourire.
Il apprenait à vivre sans entraves,
déclarait que cela simplifiait bien les choses,
me montrait qu'il m'aimait en m'offrant une tablette de Juicy-Fruit
que je fourrais dans ma bouche,
et dont la douceur ne m'a jamais quittée.

Shadow Boxes

In a box, in the upstairs closet at my parents' house, are
photographs taken before I was born.

The sepia-prints, with gold-green hues, are surreal
painted versions of the parents I know.

By the time I met them, they were more settled,
past their carefree twenties.

My parents were not hippies, so these photos are
their only tie-dyed relics.

Some of the photos have blood-soaked edges, from
being in my father's wallet when the car-jack

gave way and crushed his leg in Panama.
But that didn't save him from going to Vietnam.

My mother smiling, looks serene and beautiful,
with that halo of brownish-red, encircling her head,

as if waiting for my father, four-times she waited, to
return from the lush jungle

of camouflage green, and gun-metal gray,
with fogs of agent-orange blocking out the sun.

Schaukästen

In einer Schachtel im Obergeschoss meines Elternhauses
ruhen Fotos, die vor meiner Geburt gemacht wurden.

Die Sepia-Drucke, mit gold-grünen Farbtönen, sind surreal
gemalte Versionen der Eltern, die ich kenne.

Zu der Zeit, als ich sie kennenlernte, waren sie eher gesetzt,
lang nach ihren sorgenfreien Zwanzigern.

Meine Eltern waren keine Hippies, daher sind diese Bilder
ihre einzigen gebatikten Überbleibsel.

Manche der Fotos haben blutgetränkte Ränder,
da sie sich in der Brieftasche meines Vaters befanden, als der
    Wagenheber

nachgab und sein Bein in Panama zerschmetterte.
Das bewahrte ihn jedoch nicht davor, nach Vietnam zu müssen.

Meine Mutter, lächelnd, sieht besonnen und wunderschön aus
mit diesem bräunlich roten Heiligenschein, der ihren Kopf umgibt,

als ob sie auf meinen Vater warten würde, viermal wartete sie
auf seine Rückkehr aus dem dichten Dschungel,

geprägt von Camouflagegrün und Waffenmetallgrau
mit Nebeln aus Agent-Orange, die die Sonne blockieren.

Boîtes à souvenirs

Dans une boîte du placard de l'étage chez mes parents,
il y a des photographies prises avant ma naissance.

Les tirages sépia, teintés vert et or, sont des variations
colorisées et surréalistes des parents que je connais.

À l'époque où j'entrai dans leur vie, ils étaient déjà plus rangés,
au-delà de l'insouciance de leurs vingt ans.

Mes parents n'étaient pas des hippies, ces photos sont
les seuls souvenirs façon tie-dye de ces années-là.

Certains clichés aux bords maculés de sang,
étaient dans le portefeuille de mon père, le jour où le cric

lâcha et écrasa sa jambe à Panama.
Cela ne l'exempta d'ailleurs pas d'un tour au Vietnam.

Ma mère souriante, belle et sereine,
avec ce halo de cheveux brun-roux lui auréolant la tête,

semble attendre – quatre fois elle attendit –
que mon père revienne de cette jungle luxuriante

aux tons de camouflage vert et gris d'arme-à-feu,
aux brumes d'agent Orange oblitérant le soleil.

Hester speaks

    1.

Listen child,
to what you imagine I know
to memories you do not have –
me lying beside Settindown Creek
before the cotton mill's wheel
began churning the water
before the white man
stole me from the past
and built the covered bridge
before I was old enough
to know my Cherokee name
formed from dancing spirits
that call me on the wind.

    2.

Even without memory,
I knew I should never
cut my hair –
so I grew it past the hips
that birthed a line to you
kept it in two tight braids
I would tie together
across my waist
the ends hanging loose
between my legs
thickly woven, separate lives

    3.

I do not remember
how I learned
to dance
a cup and saucer
filled with well-water

balanced on my head
how I managed
not to spill anything
why I did it the first time
why I continued

    4.

My Christian name
was a mistake
a misspelling of Esther,
another foreign bride.
She knew her real name –
Hadassah was careful
about revealing herself
but had memories, choices –
I did not marry a king
could not save my people

    5.

When you dance, child,
do you feel me?
I've watched you
spin wildly
unafraid
unashamed
unaware
it is me you hear,
my cup tipping over,
whispering a new name
for the rhythms
you cannot resist.

Hester spricht

1.

Höre, Kind,
auf Dinge, von denen du glaubst, ich wüsste sie,
auf Erinnerungen, die du nicht besitzt –
wie ich am Settindown Creek liege
bevor das Rad der Baumwollspinnerei
begann das Wasser aufzuwühlen
bevor der weiße Mann
mich aus der Vergangenheit gestohlen
und die überdachte Brücke gebaut hat
bevor ich alt genug war
meinen Cherokee-Namen zu kennen
geformt aus tanzenden Geistern,
die mich im Winde rufen.

2.

Selbst ohne Erinnerung
wusste ich, ich sollte nie
mein Haar schneiden –
also ließ ich es über meine Hüften wachsen
die eine Linie bis zu dir gebaren
trug es in zwei strammen Zöpfen
die ich zusammenband
über meiner Taille
die Enden locker herunterhängend
zwischen meinen Beinen
dicht verflochten, getrennte Leben

3.

Ich erinnere mich nicht
wie ich lernte
zu tanzen
eine Tasse mit Unterteller
gefüllt mit Brunnenwasser

auf meinem Kopf zu balancieren
wie ich es schaffte
nichts zu verschütten
warum ich es das erste Mal tat
warum ich weitermachte

    4.

Mein christlicher Name
war ein Fehler
Esther, falsch buchstabiert,
noch eine fremde Braut.
Sie wusste ihren wahren Namen –
Hadassah war vorsichtig,
wem sie sich offenbarte
aber sie hatte Erinnerungen, eine Wahl –
Ich heiratete keinen König
konnte mein Volk nicht retten

    5.

Wenn du tanzt, Kind,
fühlst du mich dann?
Ich hab' dir zugesehen
wie wild du dich drehst
ohne Angst
ohne Scham
ohne, dass du wusstest,
dass ich es bin, die du hörst,
meine Tasse, die umkippt,
flüstere einen neuen Namen
für die Rhythmen
denen du nicht widerstehen kannst.

Ainsi parle Hester

1.

Écoute, mon enfant,
ce que tu crois que je sais,
ces souvenirs qui ne sont pas les tiens –
Moi, allongée au bord de Settindown Creek
avant que la roue à aubes de la filature de coton
ne se mette à battre l'eau en écume
avant que l'homme blanc
ne me ravisse du passé
et ne bâtisse le pont couvert,
avant même que j'atteigne l'âge
de connaître le nom cherokee
créé pour moi par des esprits dansants
me hélant dans le vent.

2.

Bien que sans mémoire,
je savais que jamais il ne fallait
me couper les cheveux –
je les laissai donc pousser plus bas que ces hanches
qui allaient engendrer ta lignée,
les retenant en deux nattes serrées
liées l'une à l'autre
en travers de ma taille,
leurs extrémités libres
entre mes jambes,
vies étroitement entrelacées, vies séparées.

3.

Je ne me souviens pas
comment j'ai appris
à danser,
une soucoupe et sa tasse
remplie d'eau du puits

en équilibre sur ma tête,
comment j'arrivais
à ne rien renverser,
pourquoi un jour je me mis à danser
pourquoi j'ai continué.

    4.

Mon nom chrétien,
une erreur,
un prénom mal épelé, Esther,
une autre épouse étrangère.
Elle, connaissait son vrai nom –
Hadassah ne se dévoilait
qu'avec prudence
mais elle avait des souvenirs, des choix –
Moi, je n'ai ni épousé de roi
ni pu sauver mon peuple.

    5.

Quand tu danses, petite,
sens-tu ma présence ?
Je t'ai regardée
tournoyer sans retenue
sans peur
sans honte
sans avoir conscience
que c'est moi que tu entends,
ma tasse se renversant,
moi, te chuchotant un nom nouveau
pour ces rythmes
auxquels tu ne sais résister.

Part of the Bargain

"Take a shiny quarter for it?"
she clutched my left ring finger
caressing the wart I wanted rid of.
She had an eye twitch
as if a rapid wink had possessed her.
I couldn't imagine why
this old crone would want my wart
how exactly she would get it,
but I was thirteen and desperate,
tired of the cute boys, ugly ones too,
saying I was out kissing frogs,
calling me a witch.
So, when Granny offered
to sneak me over to the conjure woman
while my mama was running errands
I was game, eager even,
just didn't realize I'd be selling
a part of myself.

Standing there on that back porch
overhanging a creek,
I could hear the croaking
as I took the quarter
and one last look at my wart.
"Belongs to me now, quit your looking."
Her eye no longer twitched.
She turned back into her shack,
and Papa drove us home.
Next day, the wart was gone
and for the first time in my life
I felt I'd sold out,
gave away my magic for nearly nothing.

Der Preis

„Verkaufst du sie für einen glänzenden Vierteldollar?"
Sie umklammerte meinen linken Ringfinger,
streichelte die Warze, die ich loswerden wollte.
Eines ihrer Augen tanzte
wie besessen von einem wilden Zucken.
Ich konnte mir nicht vorstellen, warum
die Alte meine Warze wollte,
wie genau sie Besitz von ihr nehmen würde,
aber ich war dreizehn und verzweifelt,
genervt von allen Jungs, süß und hässlich,
die sagten, ich würde Frösche küssen und
die mich eine Hexe nannten.
Also, als Oma mir anbot,
mich heimlich zur Heilerin zu bringen,
während meine Mutter Besorgungen machte,
schlug ich ein, mehr als bereit,
nichtsahnend, dass ich
einen Teil von mir selbst verkaufen würde.

Hier auf der hinteren Veranda,
direkt über einem Quell,
konnte ich das Quaken hören,
als ich den Vierteldollar nahm
und einen letzten Blick auf meine Warze warf.
„Sie ist nun mein, hör' auf zu glotzen!"
Ihr Auge tanzte nicht länger.
Sie ging zurück in ihre Hütte,
und Opa fuhr uns nach Hause.
Am nächsten Tag war die Warze verschwunden.
Zum ersten Mal in meinem Leben
fühlte ich mich, als hätte ich meine Seele verkauft,
meine Magie verschenkt, für nichts und wieder nichts.

Un marché de dupes

« Tu m'l'échanges contre une belle pièce de 25 cents? »
Elle agrippait mon annulaire gauche
tout en caressant la verrue dont je voulais me débarrasser.
Sa paupière tressautait,
comme sous l'emprise d'un tic incontrôlable.
Je n'arrivais pas à comprendre pourquoi
cette vieille chouette convoitait ma verrue,
ni comment elle comptait s'y prendre pour me l'enlever,
mais j'avais treize ans et j'étais désespérée,
j'en avais assez des garçons mignons, comme des moches d'ailleurs,
qui racontaient que je n'étais qu'une embrasseuse de grenouilles,
me traitaient de sorcière.
Alors, quand Granny m'a proposé
d'aller voir la passeuse en cachette
pendant que ma maman faisait ses emplettes,
j'étais pour, enthousiaste même,
je ne me rendais simplement pas compte que j'allais troquer
une partie de moi-même.

À l'arrière de la maison, sur ce porche
surplombant un ruisseau
l'oreille pleine du coassement des grenouilles,
Je saisis la pièce de monnaie
et jetai un dernier coup d'oeil à ma verrue.
« Elle est mienne maintenant, bas les yeux! »
L'œil calme et débarrassé de son tic,
elle s'en retourna dans sa cahute,
et grand-papa nous ramena en voiture à la maison.
Le jour suivant, la verrue avait disparu
et pour la première fois de ma vie,
j'eus le sentiment d'avoir fait un marché de dupes,
d'avoir bradé ma magie.

Emma's Tattoo

With his fingers tracing lightly across my chest,
he kissed me, stood and adjusted his tie.
Pausing in the doorway, he smiled,
before disappearing down the hall.

On the way to the bathroom,
I stopped in front of the mirror –
Massaging my nipples
between forefinger and thumb
pressing up with my palms,
to create more cleavage.

"This will be uncomfortable," the nurse said.
I willed myself not to scream
when the metal plates pressed,
pressed unmercifully,
until I thought my breasts would explode.

When the technician came
to mark me for radiation
I asked him to make little flowers.
He wouldn't look at me,
"I only have green ink."

Afterwards, the counselor told me not to look.
On the eighth day, after my husband
brought roses, yellow, not red,
I locked myself in the bathroom,
pulled away the bandages, and mourned.

Six months later, I drive
to the outskirts of town
to a rundown store with motorcycles parked in front.
"Yeah, sure honey, no problem,"
the woman wearing a studded leather corset
nods at my drawing of a forget-me-not.
When I pull open my blouse,

the woman with a dragon
climbing from her cleavage,
crosses her arms tight,
stumbles backward, and winces.

Emmas Tattoo

Während seine Finger leicht über meine Brust wanderten,
küsste er mich, stand auf und richtete seine Krawatte.
Im Türrahmen hielt er inne und lächelte,
bevor er im Flur verschwand.

Auf dem Weg ins Badezimmer
stoppte ich vor dem Spiegel –
massierte meine Brustwarzen
zwischen Zeigefinger und Daumen
und drückte meine Brüste nach oben,
um mehr Dekolleté zu schaffen.

„Das wird jetzt etwas unangenehm", sagte die Krankenschwester.
Ich zwang mich nicht zu schreien,
als die Metallplatten drückten,
unbarmherzig drückten,
bis ich dachte, meine Brüste würden platzen.

Als der Radiologieassistent kam,
um mich für die Bestrahlung zu markieren,
bat ich ihn, Blümchen zu malen.
Er schaute mich nicht an,
„Ich habe nur grüne Farbe."

Danach sagte mir die Therapeutin, ich solle nicht hinsehen.
Am achten Tag, nachdem mir mein Mann
Rosen mitbrachte, gelbe, keine roten,
schloss ich mich ins Badezimmer ein,
zog die Verbände weg und trauerte.

Sechs Monate später fahre ich an den Stadtrand
zu einem heruntergekommenen Laden mit davor geparkten
    Motorrädern.
„Na klar, Süße, kein Problem",
die Frau im nietenbesetzten Lederkorsett
nickt beim Blick auf meine Zeichnung eines Vergissmeinnichts.
Ich knöpfe meine Bluse auf,
und die Frau, der ein Drache
aus dem Ausschnitt klettert,
schreckt zurück
und verschränkt ihre Arme fest vor der Brust.

La tatouage d'Emma

Traçant du bout des doigts un chemin sur ma poitrine,
Il m'embrassa, se leva et ajusta sa cravate.
Il s'immobilisa dans l'embrasure de la porte, me sourit
avant de disparaître dans le couloir.

Sur le chemin de la salle de bain,
Je fis face du miroir –
massant mes mamelons
entre le pouce et l'index
soulevant mes seins à pleines mains,
pour les faire pigeonner.

« Cela va être désagréable », dit l'infirmière.
Je m'interdis de crier
quand les plaques en métal pressèrent,
pressèrent sans pitié,
tant que je crus mes seins allaient éclater.

Quand le technicien arriva
pour me marquer pour la radiation
Je lui demandai de dessiner des petites fleurs.
Il refusa de croiser mon regard,
« Je n'ai que de l'encre verte ».

Après, la thérapeute me conseilla de ne pas regarder.
Le huitième jour, après la visite mon mari
qui m'apporta des roses jaunes, pas des rouges,
je m'enfermai dans la salle de bain,
je retirai les pansements et pleurai ce que j'avais perdu.

Six mois plus tard, je me rends en voiture
aux abords de la ville
jusqu'à un salon vétuste avec des motos en stationnement.
« Ouais, OK chérie, pas de problème », la femme corsetée de cuir
    clouté
hoche la tête devant mon dessin symbolique d'un brin de myosotis.
Quand j'ouvre les pans de mon corsage,
la femme au dragon tatoué
remontant de son décolleté, recule,
chancelante, visage crispé,
et se protège la poitrine de ses bras croisés.

Instructions for my Burial Clothes

Sometimes I dream
Dolly Parton is my aunt.
I'm about twelve.
She comes to visit
at Easter,
brings me chocolates,
jelly beans
and makeup.

My mother frowns,
hurries around the kitchen
with other female relatives –
they are all wearing sackcloth. Dolly sits
beside me,
plays a guitar and sings, her long
red-glittered nails click against
the frets.

When I say,
"Do not bury me in a suit,
I want to go out in sequins," my
mother shakes her head,
wonders where I learned such excess.

Anweisungen für meinen Abgesang

Manchmal träume ich,
Dolly Parton wäre meine Tante.
Ich bin etwa zwölf.
Sie kommt zu Besuch,
an Ostern,
bringt mir Schokolade,
Jelly Beans und Schminke.

Meine Mutter runzelt die Stirn,
eilt durch die Küche

mit anderen weiblichen Verwandten –
sie alle tragen Kittelschurz.
Dolly sitzt neben mir,
spielt Gitarre und singt,
ihre langen rot glitzernden
Nägel klacken gegen die Bünde.

Wenn ich sage,
„Beerdigt mich nicht traditionell,
ich möchte in Pailletten abtreten",
schüttelt meine Mutter ihren Kopf,
und wundert sich, wo ich solchen Exzess
gelernt habe.

Consignes sur le choix de ma tenue funéraire

Dans mes rêves de temps en temps
Dolly Parton est ma tante.
J'ai environ douze ans.
Elle nous rend visite
à Pâques,
m'apporte des chocolats,
des Jelly beans
et du maquillage.

Ma mère, sourcils froncés,
s'affaire dans la cuisine
avec quelques femmes de la famille –
toutes sont habillées de toile de coton usagée*
Dolly est assise
à mes côtés,
elle joue de la guitare et chante,
Ses longs ongles rouges brillants
Cliquètent sur les frettes.

Quand je déclare,
« Je t'interdis de m'inhumer en tailleur,
je veux tirer ma révérence en tenue à paillettes »,
ma mère ne peut que hocher la tête,
se demande d'où me vient ce goût pour l'extravagance.

---

*Sackcloth : Littéralement "toile à sac". Le poète fait ici référence à la réutilisation, dans les ménages modestes, de la toile en coton imprimé des sacs de farine ou même de nourriture à bestiaux pour se faire des robes. Cette pratique est particulièrement représentative des années qui vont de la Grande Dépression à la fin de la deuxième guerre mondiale dans les campagnes américaines ou canadiennes.

My Paris Year Trois

Under the influence of Frank O'Hara and Mina Loy

Bruce Willis held the door for me at Chanel
a story that should stand on its own merits
or lack thereof, except that later, at dinner,
after I regale everyone with my "famous person" story
Martina begins to discuss the beauty
of *Notre Dame*, the church not the woman,
except it really is about the woman
because what we are questioning
is spirituality itself, and I say,
Even a self-professed atheist should be moved
but Andrew hears, *Even a sock-wearing atheist,*
and we laugh, except there is an air of something
unsaid, something perhaps about what it means
to be moved, so Jay and Maria make a joke
about coq au vin always sounding pornographic,
which we all agree, not being French,
is appropriately French, except *coq* is cock
in our language, the American sound being
a large part of what seems illicit, which isn't
the same as explicit, something we are all
trying to be, but failing to do,
particularly exceptional when you consider
that words are our vocation –
if this were one century earlier,
the men would escort us to our hotel
leave us alone with our prayers
head for *Montmartre's Cabaret du Neant*
hold the door open for sin –
instead, I order another round of Kir,
thrust my right pinky into the candle flame,
shake loose my hair, find any temptation
entirely my own.

Mein Jahr in Paris Trois

Unter dem Einfluss von Frank O'Hara und Mina Loy

Bruce Willis hielt für mich bei Chanel die Tür auf,
eine Geschichte, die ihre eigenen Vorzüge hat
oder auch nicht, außer dass später, beim Dinner,
nachdem ich jeden mit meiner „Promi"-Geschichte unterhalten habe,
Martina über die Schönheit
von *Notre Dame* diskutiert, die Kirche, nicht die Frau,
aber eigentlich geht es doch um die Frau,
denn was wir hier in Frage stellen,
ist Spiritualität an sich, und ich sage,
Sogar ein selbsterklärter Atheist wäre davon bewegt,
aber Andrew versteht, *Sogar ein sockentragender Atheist,*
und wir lachen, nur liegt da etwas in der Luft,
ungesagt, vielleicht darüber, was es bedeutet,
bewegt zu sein, also reißen Jay und Maria einen Witz
über Coq au Vin und seinen unanständigen Klang,
dem wir, keine Franzosen, zustimmen,
denn es ist typisch französisch, nur dass *coq* ‚cock' ist
in unserer Sprache, der amerikanische Klang
doch scheinbar zweideutig, was nicht
dasselbe ist wie eindeutig, was wir alle
sein wollen, aber nicht können,
besonders bemerkenswert, wenn man bedenkt,
dass Worte unsere Berufung sind –
lebten wir ein Jahrhundert früher,
würden uns die Männer zu unserem Hotel eskortieren,
uns mit unseren Gebeten allein lassen,
sich auf den Weg machen zu *Montmartres Cabaret du Neant*
und die Tür weit offenhalten für die Sünde –
stattdessen bestelle ich noch eine Runde Kir,
stoße meinen kleinen Finger in die Kerzenflamme,
schüttele mein Haar auf, begegne meinen Versuchungen ganz
für mich allein.

Mon Paris – Trois

Écrit sous l'influence de Frank O'Hara et Mina Loy

Bruce Willis m'a tenu la porte chez Chanel,
une anecdote qui, en elle-même vaudrait,
ou non d'être racontée, sauf que plus tard, au dîner,
après avoir régalé tout le monde de mon histoire « people »,
Martina se met à deviser sur la beauté
de *Notre Dame*, l'église, pas la femme,
sauf que c'est bien de la femme dont il s'agit
car ce que nous remettons en question
c'est l'essence même de la spiritualité et je dis,
Même un athéiste autoproclamé devrait être touché
mais Andrew comprend *même un athéiste socquettes aux pieds,*
et ça nous fait rire, sauf qu'il y a comme
un non-dit, peut-être sur ce que cela veut dire
d'être touché, et alors Jay et Maria font une blague
sur le coq au vin et son invariable consonance licencieuse,
ce qui, nous tombons tous d'accord, n'étant pas Français,
est français par excellence, sauf que coq est *cock*
dans notre langue, l'inflexion américaine
en grande partie responsable de ce qui semble illicite, ce qui est
très différent d'explicite, ce que nous nous efforçons tous
d'être, sans grand succès,
tout-à-fait paradoxal quand on considère
que les mots sont notre vocation –
Un siècle plus tôt,
les hommes nous auraient escortées à notre hôtel,
abandonnées à nos dévotions
et auraient pris le chemin du *Cabaret du Néant de Montmartre*
ouvrant la porte à la débauche –
Mais aujourd'hui, je commande une nouvelle tournée de Kir,
perce la flamme de la bougie de mon petit doigt,
libère ma chevelure, et découvre que moi seule suis maîtresse
de toutes les tentations.

Day Trip:
My Friend Randi Suggests a New Post

Despite my lack of German and funds,
I have decided to take a friend's advice,
and become the poet laureate of Dortmund.

I expect to find myself on the run,
expatriates always survive by some device,
despite a lack of German and funds.

Will homeland security require a special form?
Perhaps there will be an untold price
for becoming the poet laureate of Dortmund?

Such aspirations can't be the norm,
perhaps it is a kind of literary avarice –
attribute it to my lack of German and funds.

Images of Eliot, Pound, and Stein overcome
my commonsense. I'm so easily enticed
to wish myself the poet laureate of Dortmund.

No doubt there will be those who are stunned
(no one who knows me will be surprised)
that despite my lack of German and funds
I want to become the poet laureate of Dortmund.

Tagesausflug:
Meine Freundin Randi schlägt mir einen neuen Posten vor

Trotz meines Mangels an Deutsch und Erspartem
habe ich entschieden, den Rat einer Freundin anzunehmen
und die Stadtdichterin von Dortmund zu werden.

Ich sehe mich schon auf und davon,
Auswanderer überleben immer irgendwie
trotz Mangels an Deutsch und Erspartem.

Brauche ich für den Grenzschutz ein besonderes Formular?
Vielleicht wird es einen ungeahnten Preis geben dafür,
die Stadtdichterin von Dortmund zu werden?

Solche Ambitionen können nicht die Norm sein,
vielleicht ist es eine Art literarische Habgier –
schreibt es meinem Mangel an Deutsch und Erspartem zu.

Bilder von Eliot, Pound und Stein überwältigen
mein Urteilsvermögen. Ich bin so leicht verleitet,
mir zu wünschen, die Stadtdichterin von Dortmund zu sein.

Zweifellos werden einige sprachlos sein
(niemand, der mich kennt, wäre überrascht),
dass ich trotz meines Mangels an Deutsch und Erspartem
die Stadtdichterin von Dortmund werden will.

Excursion d'un jour:
Mon amie Randi me suggère un nouveau poste

Faisant fi de mon pauvre allemand et mon manque d'argent,
je choisis de suivre l'avis d'une amie,
et de briguer les lauriers de poète de D.*

Je m'attends à me retrouver en cavale
mais les expatriés parviennent toujours à s'en tirer,
malgré leur pauvre allemand et leur manque d'argent.

Les aurorités de sécurité exigeront-elles des papiers particuliers?
Peut-être y aura-t-il quelque prix à payer
pour devenir le poète lauré de D?

De telles aspirations sont sûrement hors norme,
Peut-être une manière de cupidité littéraire –
Attribuez-la à mon pauvre allemand et mon manque d'argent.

Des visions d'Eliot, Pound et de Stein musèlent
mon sens commun. Je me laisse si facilement appâter
par le désir de devenir le poète lauré de D.

Nul doute d'aucuns seront abasourdis
(de mes proches, personne ne sera surpris)
que malgré mon pauvre allemand et mon manque d'argent
j'ambitionne les lauriers de poète de D.

---

* « D » pour Dortmund en Allemagne. Pour souligner le ton ludique de ce poème et me permettre de jouer avec les rimes, j'ai fait le choix de n'utiliser que l'initiale de la ville.

Guilty: A Valentine

Established in Paris on Valentine's Day in 1400, the High Court of Love dealt with love contracts, betrayals, and violence between lovers. Women selected judges on the basis of a poetry recitation.

When the woman takes the stand, demands
a hearing, some remedy,
it is because she can think of no other
way to withdraw moonlit declarations. Tokens of love
(letters, a lock of hair,
a silver charm, a pressed rose)
now mere exhibits, corroboration
of feelings she believed were true, just reminders of
what she wanted when she tried to surrender her heart.

Poetry is central: proof & judge.
That she wrote it makes it all the more damning.

Schuldig: Ein Valentinsgedicht

Gegründet am Valentinstag 1400 in Paris, befasste sich das Hohe Gericht der Liebe mit Liebesverträgen, Verrat und Gewalt zwischen Liebenden. Frauen ernannten Richterinnen aufgrund eines Gedichtvortrags.

Wenn die Frau den Zeugenstand betritt, eine
Anhörung fordert, ein Rechtsmittel,
liegt es daran, dass sie keinen anderen
Weg sieht, bei Mondschein geflüsterte Gelübde zurückzuziehen. Zeichen der
    Liebe
(Briefe, eine Haarlocke,
ein Silberamulett, eine gepresste Rose),
jetzt nur noch Beweisstücke, Indizien
für einst wahr geglaubte Gefühle, nur Erinnerungen dessen,
was sie wollte, als sie versuchte,
ihr Herz hinzugeben.

Poesie ist wesentlich: Beweis und Richter.
Dass sie dies schrieb, macht es noch vernichtender.

Preuve à charge: un billet de la Saint-Valentin*

Établie à Paris le jour de la Saint-Valentin de l'an 1400, la « Cour d'amour » se penchait sur les contrats d'amour, les trahisons et la violence entre amants. Les femmes sélectionnaient des juges sur la base d'une lecture de poèmes.

Femme, quand tu viens à la barre,
demande à être entendue, demande réparation,
c'est parce que tu ne vois pas d'autre
recours que de rétracter des promesses faites au clair de lune.
Tes gages d'amour (des lettres, une boucle de cheveux,
une breloque en argent, une rose séchée)
désormais réduites à l'état de preuves, la corroboration
de sentiments auxquels tu croyais, de simples rappels
de ce que tu désirais quand tu aspirais à offrir ton coeur.

La poésie est tout: à la fois évidence et juge.
Née de ta plume, la preuve n'en sera que plus accablante.

---

* I made the choice to go from the description of a case in front of the High Court of Love to addressing directly the woman pleading in front of the Court.

May Day

Magic arrives on the first
firefly's wings, part day, part
night, the flashing
keeps children, long past bedtime,
at partly open windows, bundled in
blankets. Winter still restrains
the night, forces inevitable slumber –
but in the air, already
the scent of cut fescue
the taste of wild blackberries,
the itch of summer creeps along
bared feet, ready to jump, ready to fly,
each night's dreams roused by
coming sunlight.

Erster Mai

Magie erscheint auf den ersten
Glühwürmchenflügeln, halb Tag, halb Nacht, das
Funkeln hält Kinder, lange nach ihrer Schlafenszeit,
an halboffenen Fenstern, eingekuschelt in Decken.
Der Winter umklammert noch
die Nacht, erzwingt unvermeidliches Schlummern –
aber in der Luft bereits
der Geruch von geschnittenem Gras,
der Geschmack von wilden Brombeeren,
das Kribbeln von Sommer kriecht entlang
entblößter Füße, bereit zu springen, bereit zu fliegen,
die Träume jeder Nacht wach gerüttelt vom
kommenden Sonnenlicht.

Jour de Mai

La magie arrive sur les ailes
de la première luciole, mi-diurne, mi-nocturne,
son clignotement
garde les enfants, bien après l'heure du coucher,
près des fenêtres entrouvertes, dans le cocon
des couvertures.
L'hiver retient encore
la nuit, précipite l'inévitable assoupissement –
mais dans l'air déjà
les senteurs d'herbe coupée
la saveur des mûres sauvages,
les picotements de l'été le long de
la peau nue de pieds, prêts à sauter, prêts à voler,
les rêves de chaque nuit ravivés par
l'aube naissante.

Cleaning Out the Pantry

New Year's Day, 2009

It begins when I decide
to pull the vanilla-bean-pod
from the sugar bowl
as I am sweetening
my morning cup of tea.

Today I return to the earth
what I have taken,
but have not used.
As sunlight edges the horizon,
cuts into the mist,
I sow *grains of paradise*
near the rose bush,
scatter *thyme* on oak tree roots,
sweep *allspice* under the porch.

Parisian Bonnes Herbes,
Chinese Five-Spice,
Madras Curry,
Hungarian Paprika:
these I swirl around me
(good luck for travel).
The neighborhood cats,
suspicious of my shabby robe,
judge my unkempt hair.
Mine is a cold but colorful ceremony,
each glass jar tapped empty,
then a quick puff of warm breath
to shake loose the dregs.

Finally, wanting
to hold something
of sunsets past –
The *saffron* I keep.

Vorräte aussortieren

Neujahrstag 2009

Es fängt an als ich beschließe
die Vanilleschote
aus dem Zuckertopf zu ziehen
während ich
meinen Morgentee süße.

Heute gebe ich der Erde zurück, was ich
genommen,
aber nicht benutzt habe.
Als sich die ersten Sonnenstrahlen über den Horizont schieben,
den Dunst durchschneiden,
säe ich *Paradieskörner*
nahe dem Rosenbusch,
verstreue *Thymian* auf Eichenwurzeln,
fege *Piment* unter die Veranda.

Kräuter der Provence,
chinesische Fünf Gewürze,
Madras Curry,
ungarischer Paprika:
sie alle wirble ich um mich herum
(das bringt Glück fürs Reisen).
Die Nachbarskatzen
misstrauen meinem schäbigen Morgenmantel,
beäugen mein unfrisiertes Haar.
Meine ist eine kalte, aber farbenfrohe Zeremonie, jedes Glas
leer geklopft,
dann ein kurzer Stoß warmen Atems, um
den Bodensatz zu lösen.

Letztendlich will ich
etwas von vergangenen
Sonnenuntergängen bewahren –
Den *Safran* behalte ich.

En rangeant le garde-manger

Jour de l'An 2009

Tout commence quand je décide
de retirer la gousse de vanille
du sucre
que je suis en train de mettre
dans ma tasse de thé matinale.

Aujourd'hui est le jour où je restitue à la terre
ce que je lui ai emprunté
mais n'ai pas utilisé.
Alors que le soleil ourle l'horizon, transperce la brume de ses rayons,
je sème les *graines de paradis*,
au pied du rosier,
éparpille le *thym* sur des racines de chêne, disperse
le *piment de la Jamaïque* sous la véranda.

Les Bonnes Herbes parisiennes,
les cinq épices chinoises,
le curry de Madras,
le paprika hongrois :
toutes s'envolent en tourbillons autour de moi
(bon présage pour les voyages).
Les chats du voisinage
regardent d'un œil méfiant mon peignoir élimé,
d'un œil critique mes cheveux en bataille.
Ce petit cérémonial rien qu'à moi, est froid mais haut en couleur,
chaque pot en verre tapoté pour le vider,
puis d'une petite bouffée de mon haleine chaude
les dernières traces d'épices sont libérées.

Finalement, parce que je tiens
à préserver une trace
des couchers de soleil d'antan –
je garde le *safran*.

Living in an old flower shop

is not the most eccentric thing
I've ever done,
not really even a conscious choice
just the sort of happenstance
poverty sometimes offers.

I was twenty-two, worked three jobs,
but on Sunday afternoons
could walk a quarter mile
down a gravel road
to visit my grandparents,
sit on their porch, drink sweet tea,
eat Little Debbie oatmeal pies.

The *poet me* wants to turn all this
into metaphor, some
exceptional conceit,
but I don't remember much
about those two years,
just the empty cooler turned closet,
the broken bedroom window that sliced
my right palm from pinky to thumb,
and nightmares of chrysanthemums.

Wohnen in einem alten Blumenladen

ist nicht das Ungewöhnlichste, was ich je getan habe,
nicht mal eine bewusste Wahl,
eher die Art zufälliger Umstand,
den Armut manchmal mit sich bringt.

Ich war zweiundzwanzig, hatte drei Jobs,
aber sonntagnachmittags
konnte ich eine viertel Meile gehen,
einen Schotterweg entlang,
meine Großeltern besuchen,

auf ihrer Veranda sitzen, Eistee trinken,
Little-Debbie-Haferkekse essen.

Die *Poetin in mir* will aus all dem
eine Metapher machen, irgendeine
außergewöhnliche Allegorie,
aber ich erinnere mich nicht an viel
aus diesen zwei Jahren,

nur der leere Kühlraum als Kleiderschrank,
das zerbrochene Schlafzimmerfenster, welches
meine rechte Hand vom kleinen Finger bis zum Daumen aufschlitzte,
und Albträume von Chrysanthemen.

Vivre dans une ancienne boutique de fleuriste

n'est pas la chose la plus excentrique que j'aie jamais faite,
pas même, à vrai dire, une décision consciente,
juste la sorte d'aléa
qui va parfois de pair avec la pauvreté.

J'avais vingt-deux ans, trois emplois,
mais le dimanche après-midi
il m'arrivait de marcher un quart de mile,
sur un chemin gravillonné
pour rendre visite à mes grands-parents,
m'asseoir sous leur véranda, boire du thé sucré,
manger des biscuits « Little Debbie » à la crème d'avoine.

Le *poète en moi* veut transformer tout cela
en métaphore, en quelque
allégorie extravagante,
mais je n'ai pas grand souvenir
de ces deux années,
à part la chambre froide devenue penderie,
la vitre brisée de ma fenêtre de chambre où je m'ouvris
la paume de la main droite du pouce au petit doigt,
et des cauchemars peuplés de chrysanthèmes.

At the Albion Beatnik Bookstore

Oxford, 2011

Dennis has just insisted
I have a piece of week-old sponge cake,
(it'll go off any minute).
The strawberry filling is a little too red,
but I love his shop,
and as I take the first dry bite
I hear a young man, a student in literature,
(the Derrida a dead give-away)
say to an obviously smitten girl,
"All poets are whores."
The scent of bergamot in my tea
starts to soften my scowl,
and I notice Rossetti's *The House of Life*
wedged in the corner of the bottom shelf.
As I pull out the volume, I think,
"Really, all poets are thieves."

Dante, I cannot blame you for wanting
to repossess the poems, even if it meant
disturbing Lizzy in her Highgate grave.
You fed on her day and night
to fuel your own fantasies,
but wanting to take back your words
does not mean you loved her less –
it is not the muse's place to possess the art.
What I cannot forgive is your cowardice,
sending Charles to her grave.
It should have been you
who pulled the worm-fed leaves
from her tangled copper hair.

Im Albion Beatnik Buchladen

Oxford, 2011

Dennis hat grad drauf beharrt,
dass ich ein Stück uralten Rührkuchen esse
(es wird jeden Moment schlecht werden).
Die Erdbeerfüllung ist etwas zu rot,
aber ich liebe seinen Laden,
und als ich den ersten trockenen Bissen nehme,
höre ich einen jungen Mann, einen Literaturstudenten,
(der Derrida hat ihn verraten)
zu einem offensichtlich verknallten Mädchen sagen,
„Alle Dichter sind Huren."
Der Duft von Bergamotte in meinem Tee
beginnt meine finstere Miene zu mildern,
und ich bemerke Rossettis *Das Haus des Lebens*
eingepfercht in der unteren Ecke des Regals.
Als ich die Ausgabe herausnehme, denke ich,
„Eigentlich sind alle Dichter Diebe."

Dante, ich kann es dir nicht verübeln,
dass du die Gedichte zurückerobern wolltest,
auch wenn es bedeutet hätte,
Lizzy in ihrem Grab in Highgate zu stören.
Du hast Tag und Nacht von ihr gezehrt,
um deine eigenen Fantasien zu nähren,
aber deine Worte zurückhaben zu wollen
bedeutet nicht, dass du sie weniger geliebt hast –
die Muse hat kein Recht die Kunst zu besitzen.
Was ich nicht vergeben kann, ist deine Feigheit,
Charles zu ihrem Grab zu schicken.
Du hättest der sein sollen,
der ihr die wurmbefallenen Blätter
aus ihrem verhedderten Kupferhaar zog.

Une visite à l'Albion Beatnik

Librairie, Oxford, 2011

Dennis vient d'insister
que je prenne un morceau de génoise vieille d'une semaine,
(dernière chance avant la poubelle).
La couche de confiture de fraise est un peu trop rouge,
mais j'adore sa librairie,
et au moment où je goûte la première bouchée rassise
J'entends un jeune homme, étudiant en littérature,
(son Derrida le trahit)
dire à une fille manifestement sous le charme,
« Tous les poètes sont des putes ».
Les exhalaisons de bergamote de ma tasse de thé
détendent peu à peu ma mine irritée,
et je repère un exemplaire de « La Maison de la Vie » de Rossetti
calé dans le coin de l'étagère du bas.
Tout en extrayant le volume, je pense,
« En fait, tous les poètes sont des voleurs »

Dante, je ne peux vous reprocher d'avoir voulu
vous réapproprier les poèmes, même au prix
du repos de Lizzy dans sa tombe de Highgate.
Vous vous êtes nourri d'elle jour et nuit,
pour alimenter vos propres fantasmes,
mais le désir de reprendre vos écrits
ne diminue en rien l'amour que vous lui portiez –
Ce n'est pas le rôle de la muse d'être la gardienne de l'art.
Ce que je ne peux vous pardonner, c'est votre lâcheté
d'envoyer Charles à la tombe de votre bien-aimée.
C'est de vos propres mains
que vous auriez dû retirer les feuillets mangés aux vers
du désordre de sa chevelure cuivrée.

Lost on Purpose

In the office of lost property on Baker Street,
bins are filled with mobile phones constantly chiming and chirping.
A black velvet evening coat hangs on a beach chair,
its rhinestone buttons cast light fragments on the wall.
In one corner, an urn (half-filled with ashes, I'm told)
tops an overturned red enamel saucepan.
On the glass shelf behind the information desk,
a set of yellowed false teeth are poised to nip a marble Krishna.
There are snowshoes, Impressionist prints, a rocking horse,
a claw-foot tub overflows with books. I count seventeen garden
    gnomes.

I consider inquiring after the tiny, silver key
that opened the lacquered box I got for my eleventh birthday,
the shamrock brooch my granny gave me,
and my first amber ring – maybe they turned up here.
Perhaps I can reclaim long-lost friends, the years 1984-88,
my mother's memory. Suddenly I find myself
holding a wedding cake knife, and I shudder, goose-pimply,
when I notice the engraved "K."
Some things, I remember, are lost on purpose.

Mit Absicht verloren

Im Fundbüro in der Baker Street
stehen Eimer voller Mobiltelefone, singen und klingen pausenlos,
ein Abendmantel aus schwarzem Samt hängt über einer Strandliege,
seine Strass-Knöpfe werfen Lichtfetzen an die Wand.
In einer Ecke thront eine Urne (halb voll mit Asche, wurde mir
    erzählt)
auf einem umgedrehten roten Emaille-Topf.
Auf dem Glasregal hinter der Auskunft
schnappt ein vergilbtes Gebiss nach einem marmornen Krishna.
Es gibt Schneeschuhe hier, impressionistische Drucke, ein
    Schaukelpferd,

eine Badewanne mit Füßen läuft über mit Büchern.
Ich zähle siebzehn Gartenzwerge.

Ich überlege, nach dem kleinen silbernen Schlüssel zu fragen,
der das lackierte Kästchen öffnete, welches ich zum elften Geburtstag
    bekam,
nach der Glücksklee-Brosche, die meine Oma mir gab,
und nach meinem ersten Bernstein-Ring – womöglich sind sie hier
    aufgetaucht.
Vielleicht kann ich lang verlorene Freunde zurückfordern, die Jahre
    1984-88,
das Gedächtnis meiner Mutter. Plötzlich sehe ich mich
ein Hochzeitstortenmesser halten und ich schaudere, gänsehäutig,
als ich das eingravierte „K" bemerke.
Einige Dinge, erinnere ich mich, werden mit Absicht verloren.

Égarées à dessein

Au bureau des objets trouvés de Baker Street,
des corbeilles entières de portables bourdonnent et carillonnent sans
    cesse.
Un manteau de soirée en velours noir est drapé sur une chaise de plage,
ses boutons de strass projettent des prismes de lumière sur le mur.
Dans un coin, une urne (à moitié remplie de cendres, me dit-on)
trône sur le cul d'une petite casserole en émail rouge.
Sur l'étagère en verre derrière le guichet d'information,
un dentier s'apprête à planter ses dents jaunies dans un Krishna de
    marbre.
Il y a des raquettes de neige, des gravures impressionnistes, un cheval à
    bascule,
une baignoire à pattes de lion débordante de livres. Je dénombre dix-
    sept nains de jardin.

Je songe à m'enquérir de la minuscule clef en argent,
qui ouvrait la boîte en laque reçue pour mes onze ans,
de la broche en forme de trèfle héritée de Granny,
et de ma première bague en pierre d'ambre – auraient-elles échoué ici
    par hasard?

Peut-être puis-je recouvrer des amitiés depuis longtemps oubliées,
les années 1984-88,
la mémoire de ma mère. Je me retrouve soudain
un couteau de gâteau de mariage à la main et suis saisie de frissons, de
    chair de poule,
quand j'y découvre, engravée, la lettre « K ».
Certaines choses, il m'en souvient, sont égarées à dessein.

To the Roses of Auvillar

1: Ronsard Pinks

Grandmothers interlocking thorny arms, heavy
from the weight of old beauty.
They could tumble, but hold each other
steady with omniscience,
overhang cobbled walls,
watch our every step.

2: White

Hint of dull jade in your complexion,
the never-married cousin of the Garonne –
easily overlooked
behind the garrulous fuchsia.
Village cats brush their heads against you,
and other people's children
clutch you to their chests before Sunday dinner.

3: Red

Being the pretty sister is never easy:
everyone wants you at their table,
expects splendor and grace,
feels free to embrace you,
take in your fragrance –
abandons you the moment
you deign to wither a mote.

4: Yellow

The baby sister, you cannot decide
what you want to be, think yourself
already grown, more sunflower than rose.
You dance in river wind on lanky legs,
your petals always tousled,
wait for someone to take you away.

An die Rosen von Auvillar

1: Ronsard-Rosa

Großmütter verschränken dornige Arme, schwer
vom Gewicht der alten Schönheit.
Sie könnten straucheln, aber halten einander
fest mit Allwissenheit,
hängen über gepflasterten Wänden,
beobachten jeden unserer Schritte.

2: Weiß

Ein Stich trüber Jade in deinem Teint,
die nie verheiratete Cousine der Garonne –
leicht zu übersehen
hinter der lauten Fuchsie.
Dorfkatzen reiben ihre Köpfe an dir,
und die Kinder anderer Leute
drücken dich vor dem Sonntagsessen an ihre Brust.

3: Rot

Die hübsche Schwester zu sein ist nie einfach:
Alle wollen dich an ihrem Tisch haben,
erwarten Pracht und Anmut,
nehmen sich die Freiheit, dich zu umarmen,
deinen Duft einzuatmen –
verstoßen dich in dem Moment,
in dem du wagst, einen Hauch zu welken.

4: Gelb

Als kleine Schwester kannst du dich nicht entscheiden,
was du sein willst, denkst, du bist
schon groß, mehr Sonnenblume als Rose.
Du tanzt im Flusswind auf zarten Beinen,
deine Blütenblätter immer zerzaust,
wartest darauf, dass dich jemand mitnimmt.

Ode aux roses d'Auvillar

1: Roses Ronsard

Aïeules aux membres entrelacés, épineux,
alourdis sous le poids d'une antique beauté.
Elles pourraient s'effondrer mais se soutiennent l'une l'autre,
inébranlables dans leur sagesse
Sentinelles des murs de pierre, elles sont là,
attentives à chacun de nos pas.

2: Blanche

Un soupçon de jade vous ternit le teint,
cousine de la Garonne, jamais mariée –
facilement oubliée
derrière le fuchsia volubile.
Les chats du village vous caressent de la tête
et les enfants des autres
vous pressent contre leur poitrine avant le dîner du dimanche.

3: Rouge

Être la sœur, la jolie, le rôle n'est jamais simple:
chacun vous demande à sa table,
n'attendant rien de moins que splendeur et grâce,
se prend la liberté de vous saisir à plein bras
de vous respirer –
pour vous laisser tomber
au moindre petit laisser-aller de votre part.

4: Jaune

Petite dernière, il n'est pas facile de decider
ce que vous voulez être, vous êtes déjà
adulte, pensez-vous, plus tournesol que rose.
Vous dansez, toute en jambes, au gré du vent venu du fleuve,
vos pétales toujours ébouriffés
dans l'attente de qui viendra vous enlever.

Flight

The flash of color, green sometimes blue,
swooshes from tree to tree, and you find
it hard to convince yourself that you've seen anything.

Away from the busy streets, a colony of monk parakeets
dazzle amid the laden orange trees at Pedralbes Monastery:
in this place belief comes easy.

Mornings, if you walk up Passeig de Gràcia, the windows
of grand Modernisme apartments thrown open wide,
you imagine the flutter of escaping wings –

you almost see the ghost of a grandmother, scanning the skies,
cursing sons and daughters and grandchildren who lacked devotion,
who left the cage door open when she died.

In the shadow of Tibidabo, where tradition holds the devil
told Jesus all these things could be his
(the mountains, the sea, these beautiful birds),

I recite a prayer of hope, knowing that once I am gone
it will be hard to believe in what I cannot see.

Im Flug

Das Leuchten der Farbe, Grün, manchmal Blau,
rauscht von Baum zu Baum, und dir fällt
es schwer zu glauben, etwas gesehen zu haben.

Abseits der geschäftigen Straßen schillert ein Schwarm Mönchssittiche
inmitten der üppigen Orangenbäume am Kloster Pedralbes: An diesem
     Ort
fällt das Glauben leicht.

Morgens, wenn du den Passeig de Gràcia hinaufgehst, die Fenster
der prächtigen Modernisme-Wohnungen weit aufgerissen,
stellst du dir das Flattern fliehender Flügel vor –

siehst du beinahe den Geist einer Großmutter, wie sie den Himmel
    absucht, Söhne
und Töchter und Enkelkinder verflucht, denen es an Hingabe
    mangelte und die die
Käfigtür offenließen, als sie starb.

Im Schatten des Tibidabo, wo der Legende nach der Teufel zu
Jesus sagte, all diese Dinge könnten ihm gehören
(die Berge, das Meer, diese wunderschönen Vögel),

spreche ich ein Gebet der Hoffnung und weiß, wenn ich gegangen bin,
wird es schwer sein, an das zu glauben, was ich nicht sehen kann.

Envol

La fulgurance de couleur, verte parfois bleue,
fuse d'arbre en arbre et vous avez peine
à vous convaincre que ce n'était pas une illusion.

À l'écart des rues animées, une colonie de perruches moines
enchante l'œil parmi les orangers foisonnants du monastère de
    Pedralbes :
C'est un endroit qui vous invite à croire.

Le matin, si vous remontez le Passeig de Gràcia, les fenêtres
de ses imposants appartements modernistes grand ouvertes,
vous imaginez le bruissement d'une échappée d'ailes –

Vous pressentez le fantôme d'une aïeule scrutant les cieux,
maudissant des fils, filles et petits-enfants indifférents
qui laissèrent ouverte la porte de la cage quand elle trépassa.

À l'ombre du Tibidabo, où selon la tradition le diable
dit à Jésus que toutes ces choses alentour pouvaient être à lui
(les montagnes, la mer, ces magnifiques oiseaux),

je récite une prière d'espoir, sachant qu'une fois partie,
il me sera difficile de croire en ce que mes yeux ne peuvent voir.

What we missed

The giddy flush of young love,
we've only glimpsed a few times –
that evening in the museum
when you gave me a CD "mix-tape"
the likes of which I hadn't heard
in decades; that morning you met me
at the Dusseldorf train station,
bag thrown over your shoulder
arms wide, you lifted me off my feet,
swung me a quarter turn; that night
we drank Port until 2:00 am,
and danced our way home under fairy lights;
that afternoon we cuddled close
at the National Zoo, held your camera
at arm's length and snapped happiness.

Each morning when you bring me tea
I concede finding each other late was for the best.
Still, sometimes I mourn the years we never had
even the ones that would have destroyed us.

Was uns entging

Den flatterhaften Anflug junger Liebe
erlebten wir nur wenige Male –
an diesem Abend im Museum,
als du mir eine Mix-CD gabst
von der Art, wie ich sie seit Jahrzehnten nicht
gehört hatte; an diesem Morgen, als du mich trafst
am Düsseldorfer Hauptbahnhof,
die Tasche über deine Schulter geworfen,
die Arme weit offen, mich von meinen Füßen hobst
und mich eine Vierteldrehung schwangst; in dieser Nacht,
als wir bis um zwei Portwein tranken
und unter Lichterketten heimtanzten;
an diesem Nachmittag, als wir innig

im National Zoo kuschelten, deine Kamera
auf Armlänge hielten und Freude einfingen.

Jeden Morgen, wenn du mir Tee bringst,
gestehe ich, dass wir uns so spät trafen, war zu unserem Besten.
Trotz allem trauere ich manchmal um die Jahre, die wir nie hatten,
auch um jene, die uns hätten zerstören können.

Les années que nous n'avons pas eues

L'euphorisante ivresse du jeune amour,
nous ne l'avons connue qu'une ou deux fois –
ce soir-là au musée
quand tu m'as donné une compil' sur CD
comme je n'en avais plus entendu
depuis des décennies; le matin où tu m'as retrouvée
à la gare de Düsseldorf,
le sac sur l'épaule
les bras grand ouverts et que tu m'as soulevée de terre,
m'as fait valser un quart de tour; la nuit où
nous avons bu du Porto jusqu'à 2h du matin,
et dansé jusque chez nous, sous la lumière des guirlandes électriques;
l'après-midi où, blottis l'un contre l'autre
au National Zoo, nous avons tenu ton appareil photo
à bout de bras pour prendre l'instantané du bonheur.

Chaque matin, alors que tu m'apportes ma tasse de thé
je reconnais que nous avons eu de la chance de nous être rencontrés sur
    le tard.
Pourtant, il m'arrive de pleurer les années que nous n'avons pas eues,
même celles qui nous auraient détruits.

In my kitchen in Atlanta

for Allen Ginsberg

You do like to surprise.
So, the mornings I stumble
into the kitchen,
unprepared even to put on
the kettle, much less
face the day, only to discover
your naked body, contorting
in what you swear are Tai Chi moves,
I grapple with your eccentricities
which push beyond the surreal,
beyond the sublime,
beyond what anyone should submit
to before the sun rises.
This I could live with, Allen.
But when you begin to lose focus,
criticize my bathrobe,
scold me for eating bacon,
mock me for not writing
something important each day,
I want to tell you to take it up
with the universe – except
I know you will,
and, ultimately, I'll read some line
you wrote years before my birth
and I will feel the reproach
meant for those you knew
would be inclined to listen.
Nevertheless, you are always welcome here.
Try not to step on the cats.

In meiner Küche in Atlanta

für Allen Ginsberg

Du magst es echt zu überraschen.
Also, an den Morgen, an denen ich in die
Küche stolpere,
nicht einmal bereit den
Wasserkessel aufzusetzen, geschweige denn
es mit dem Tag aufzunehmen, nur um
deinen nackten Körper vorzufinden, der sich verdreht
in Bewegungen, die du Tai-Chi nennst,
ringe ich mit deiner Verschrobenheit, die
jenseits des Surrealen liegt,
jenseits des Sublimen,
jenseits dessen, was sich jemand vor
Sonnenaufgang antun sollte.
Damit könnte ich leben, Allen.
Aber wenn du beginnst, den Fokus zu verlieren,
meinen Bademantel zu kritisieren,
mich dafür zu tadeln, dass ich Bacon esse,
mich zu verspotten, weil ich nicht jeden Tag
etwas Wichtiges schreibe,
sag' ich dir, nimm es doch
mit dem Universum auf – aber
ich weiß, das wirst du sowieso,
und letztendlich werd' ich irgendeine Zeile lesen,
die du Jahre vor meiner Geburt geschrieben hast,
und ich werde den Vorwurf spüren
gerichtet an jene, von denen du wusstest,
sie würden dir freiwillig zuhören.
Wie dem auch sei, du bist hier immer willkommen.
Versuch' nicht auf die Katzen zu treten.

Dans ma cuisine à Atlanta

pour Allen Ginsberg

Tu prends vraiment plaisir à faire des surprises.
Alors, les matins où je me traîne
jusqu'à la cuisine,
à peine capable de mettre
la bouilloire sur le feu, encore moins
d'affronter la journée, et que je te trouve
nu, au milieu de contorsions,
qui, insistes-tu, sont des enchaînements de Tai Chi,
je peine à embrasser tes excentricités
qui vont au-delà du surréalisme,
au-delà du sublime,
au-delà de ce que quiconque
devrait avoir à endurer
avant le lever du soleil.
Tout cela je pourrais bien m'en accommoder, Allen.
Mais quand tu perds le fils de tes pensées,
que tu critiques mon peignoir de bain,
me réprimandes parce que je mange du bacon,
et me nargues de ne pas écrire
quelque chose de profond chaque jour,
J'ai bien envie de te dire de t'adresser
tout droit Là-Haut – sauf que
c'est exactement ce que tu vas faire,
et, que pour finir, je lirai quelque phrase
écrite des années avant ma naissance,
touchée par le reproche
adressé à ceux
disposés à t'écouter.
Quoi qu'il en soit, tu es toujours le bienvenu chez moi.
Évite de marcher sur les chats.

Blues Harbor

Underground Atlanta, 1990

    I: Woke up this morning with an awful aching head.

Joel and I drove downtown,
a couple of suburban kids,
our whiteness only outshone
by our greenness – but, hey,
all the yuppies were into the Blues.

AC Reed was downing milk and J&B,
said it calmed his stomach,
before he assailed us on the sax.

I told the waitress, Lisa,
that I loved her earrings,
and then, as if someone else
was talking, I heard myself say,
"That guy working the door,
do you think you could get me his number?"
A few minutes later she delivered
another margarita, said,
"Dave told me to tell you to come
get it for yourself. Y'all are cute."

Joel waited outside while I chatted up
this dark-haired stranger, told me I was crazy
on the ride home.

Dave would buy me a black fringe suede jacket
for Christmas, take me to see
the Rolling Stones at Bobby Dodd Stadium.

For a few months we would split time
between his studio at the Darlington
and my shared townhouse in Alpharetta.

Soon after he took me to meet his parents,
it would end. Even now, I try to convince myself
I can't remember why.

II: Woke up this morning with an awful aching head.

Never leave one guitar-playing bartender for another.

Hindsight is a bitch,
but that day when Jeff stepped onto
the beer cooler and jumped the bar
just tell me how fine I looked
in the black and white wrap dress
my mom bought me for Nancy's wedding
(where I was foolish enough to catch the bouquet)
I'd never felt more flattered.

For a few months, I spent hours
in the backs of bars listening
to him play: Stevie Ray's "Cold Shot"
was our song, but he didn't know it.

One night after we
had sex in the shower,
I drifted off to sleep listening
to Blind Faith singing "Can't Find My Way Home."

I should have listened more closely to the lyrics,
instead of being caught up in the rhythms.

III: My new man had left me, just a room and an empty bed.

Licking my wounds, I was becoming
just another barfly when Mark
came along to save me.
Maybe because he was the sound man,

I felt I could trust him to control things.
Everyone was pulling for us.

We got married, and bought a house –
north of Alpharetta, more suburban than ever.
We made a real go of it, and we loved each other,
in our own ways.

Still, I should have known,
that whatever begins with the blues will end there, too.

Blues Harbor

Underground Atlanta, 1990

> *I: Bin heute morgen mit schrecklichen Kopfschmerzen aufgewacht.*

Joel und ich fuhren in die Innenstadt, ein
paar Kids aus der Vorstadt,
unser Weißsein nur übertroffen
von unserer Blauäugigkeit – aber, hey, alle
Yuppies standen auf Blues.

AC Reed kippte Milch mit J&B runter, sagte,
es beruhige seinen Magen,
bevor er uns mit dem Saxophon überfiel.

Ich sagte der Kellnerin, Lisa,
dass ich ihre Ohrringe toll fand, und
dann, als ob jemand anderes
sprach, hörte ich mich selbst sagen,
„Der Türsteher da drüben,
denkst du, du kannst mir seine Nummer besorgen?"
Ein paar Minuten später brachte sie eine
neue Margarita und sagte dabei,
„Dave lässt ausrichten, du sollst
sie dir selber holen. Ihr seid putzig."

Joel wartete draußen, während ich
diesen dunkelhaarigen Fremden anquatschte, sagte mir
auf der Rückfahrt, ich sei irre.

Dave würde mir eine schwarze Wildlederjacke mit Fransen
zu Weihnachten kaufen, mich zu den
Rolling Stones im Bobby-Dodd-Stadion einladen.

Für ein paar Monate würden wir pendeln
zwischen seiner Einzimmerwohnung im Darlington und
meiner Reihenhaus-WG in Alpharetta.

Kurz nachdem er mich seinen Eltern vorgestellt hatte, würde es
enden. Sogar jetzt versuche ich mich noch davon zu
überzeugen, dass ich nicht mehr weiß, warum.

*II: Bin heute morgen mit schrecklichen Kopfschmerzen
aufgewacht.*

Verlasse niemals einen gitarrespielenden Barkeeper für einen anderen.
Hinterher ist man immer schlauer,
aber an dem Tag, als Jeff auf
den Bierkühler stieg und sich über die Bar schwang,
nur um mir zu sagen, wie gut ich aussah
in dem schwarz-weißen Wickelkleid, das

meine Mom mir für Nancys Hochzeit gekauft hatte
(wo ich dumm genug war, den Brautstrauß zu fangen),
fühlte ich mich geschmeichelt wie nie zuvor.

Einige Monate lang verbrachte ich Stunden hinten in
Bars, wo ich ihm beim
Spielen zuhörte: Stevie Rays „Cold Shot"
war unser Song, aber das wusste er nicht.

Eines Nachts, nachdem wir
Sex in der Dusche hatten,
glitt ich in den Schlaf, während ich
Blind Faith singen hörte: „Can't Find My Way Home."

Ich hätte genauer auf den Text hören sollen, anstatt mich
im Takt zu verlieren.

*III: Mein neuer Mann hatte mich zurückgelassen, nur ein Zimmer
und ein leeres Bett.*

Meine Wunden leckend wurde ich zu einem
der Kneipenhocker, als Mark
daher kam, um mich zu retten.
Vielleicht, weil er der Tontechniker war, traute ich
ihm zu, die Dinge zu kontrollieren. Alle glaubten an uns.

Wir heirateten und kauften ein Haus –
nördlich von Alpharetta, mehr Vorstadt denn je.
Wir haben es wirklich miteinander versucht, und wir haben einander
    geliebt,
auf unsere eigene Weise.

Trotzdem hätte ich wissen müssen,
dass alles, was mit dem Blues beginnt, dort auch endet.

Blues Harbor

Underground Atlanta, 1990

I: Réveil, ce matin, avec un horrible mal de tête.

Joel et moi sommes allés en voiture au centre-ville,
deux gosses des banlieues aisées,
notre naïveté encore plus claire
que notre peau blanche – mais bon,
tous les yuppies étaient des fanas de Blues.

AC Reed descendait du lait et du J&B, disait
que ça calmait son estomac,
avant de nous subjuguer avec son saxo.

J'ai dit à la serveuse, Lisa,
que j'aimais ses boucles d'oreilles,
et puis, comme si quelqu'un d'autre
avait ouvert la bouche, je me suis entendue demander,
« Ce type qui fait les entrées,
tu crois que tu pourrais m'avoir son numéro ? »
Quelques minutes plus tard, elle me servait
une autre margarita, disant, « Dave m'a dit de te dire de venir
le chercher toi-même. Vous êtes mignons tous les deux. »

Joel m'a attendu dehors pendant que je draguais
cet étranger brun, m'a dit que j'étais dingue
sur le chemin du retour.

Dave allait m'acheter une veste en daim noir à franges
pour Noël, m'emmener à un concert
des Rolling Stones au stade Bobby Dodd.

Pendant quelques mois, nous allions passer notre temps
entre son studio au Darlington
et ma maison en coloc à Alpharetta.

Peu après m'avoir présentée à ses parents,
nous allions nous séparer. Aujourd'hui encore, j'essaie de prétendre
que je ne sais pas pourquoi.

II: Réveil, ce matin, avec un horrible mal de tête.

Attention ! un barman guitariste peut en cacher un autre.
Avec le recul, ça crève les yeux,
mais ce jour-là, quand Jeff est monté
sur la glacière pour sauter par-dessus le bar
juste pour me dire combien il me trouvait jolie
dans la robe portefeuille blanche et noire,
que maman m'avait achetée pour le mariage de Nancy
(où j'ai été assez stupide pour attraper le bouquet de la mariée),
ses compliments m'ont grisée.

Pendant quelques mois j'ai passé des heures dans
le fond des bars à l'écouter
jouer: « Cold Shot » de Stevie Ray,
cette chanson c'était nous mais il n'en avait pas conscience.

Une nuit, après avoir fait l'amour sous la douche,
je me suis endormie en écoutant
Blind Faith chanter « Can't Find My Way Home ».
J'aurais dû faire plus attention aux paroles
au lieu de me laisser envoûter par les rythmes.

III: Mon nouveau mec était parti, de ma chambre et de mon lit.

Pansant mes blessures, j'étais en passe de devenir
un pilier de bar parmi d'autres quand Mark
est venu me secourir.
Peut-être parce qu'il avait la charge de la sono,
Je sentais que je pouvais lui confier les manettes.
Tout le monde croisait les doigts pour nous.

Nous nous sommes mariés et avons acheté une maison –
au nord d'Alpharetta, plus banlieue pavillonnaire que jamais
Nous y avons vraiment mis du nôtre et nous nous sommes aimés,
à notre façon.

Mais j'aurais bien dû savoir
que Blues d'un jour rime avec Blues toujours.

Olympia

Because I am a goddess
there has always
been a place for me here.
Today I stand, disguised
as an olive tree,
watching the tourists,
a few of them
seeking my shelter
from the July sun.
I tell the cicadas
to sing them a story.

A few moons from now,
Hestia's feigned virgins
will arrive to reignite
the flame at my temple –
it's all a trick of mirrors
these days. Still,
I am amused that
women, goddesses (and not),
remain the source
of so much light.

Olympia

Weil ich eine Göttin bin,
gab es hier immer
einen Platz für mich.
Heute stehe ich, in der Gestalt
eines Olivenbaums,
beobachte die Touristen,
einige von ihnen
suchen meinen Schutz
vor der Julisonne.
Ich sage den Zikaden,
sie mögen ihnen eine Geschichte singen.

In ein paar Monden
werden Hestias Scheinjungfrauen
eintreffen, um die Flamme
an meinem Tempel neu zu entfachen –
alles ist ein Spiegeltrick
heutzutage. Trotzdem
bin ich amüsiert, dass
Frauen, Göttinnen (und die, die es nicht sind),
die Quelle
von so viel Licht bleiben.

Olympie

Déesse que je suis,
j'ai toujours eu
ma place ici.
Aujourd'hui, me voici sous le masque
d'un olivier,
observant les touristes,
quelques-uns
cherchent l'abri de ma feuillée
contre le soleil de juillet.
J'invite les cigales
à leur chanter une histoire.

À quelques lunes de là,
les pseudos vierges d'Hestia
vont arriver pour ranimer
la flamme de mon temple –
un simple jeu de miroirs
de nos jours. Malgré tout,
je m'amuse du fait que
les femmes, déesses (ou pas),
demeurent la source
de tant de lumière.

Perspective

I don't know where I'm going.
But, I sure know where I've been.

It's 1987 and my new
"Fuck you, world!" anthem
is "Here I Go Again"
by Whitesnake,
which I play over and over
on the Sony DiscMan
that's riding shotgun
in my $400 (cash)
'76 Mercury Capri –

With a number
of unpredictable
and predictable
accidents ahead,
I'm shifting gears,
windows down,
cruising along
the Chattahoochee
behind Eagle's Landing
subdivision, imagining
myself as Tawny Kitaen
somersaulting
between Jaguars,
thinking the height
of success is having
a rock star with hair
bigger than mine
stick his tongue
down my throat.

Today, I write with perspective
longer than the fake nails
I used to have. I catch a replay
of the video on YouTube,
notice for the first time,

that those boys,
if you striped them,
and shaved them bald,
would fall, heavy, like Samson.
And, Tawny?
I'd teach her to write poetry –
dance naked in metaphor.

But before any
of that can happen,
my brakes will fail
and I'll slam
into an embankment
totaling what's left
of my youth.

Perspektive

I don't know where I'm going.
But, I sure know where I've been.

Es ist 1987 und meine neue
„Fuck you, world!"-Hymne
ist „Here I Go Again"
von Whitesnake,
die ich in Dauerschleife abspiele
auf dem Sony DiscMan,
meinem Beifahrer
im 400 Dollar (in bar)
teuren '76er Mercury Capri –

Mit einer Reihe
unvorhersehbarer
und vorhersehbarer
Unfälle vor mir,
wechsle ich den Gang,
die Fenster unten,
cruise entlang dem
Chattahoochee-Fluss,

hinter der Siedlung
von Eagle's Landing, stelle mir vor,
ich wäre Tawny Kitaen,
die einen Überschlag
zwischen zwei Jaguars macht
im Glauben, der Höhepunkt
des Erfolgs sei es,
wenn ein Rockstar mit
mehr Volumen im Haar
als ich selbst
seine Zunge
in meinen Hals steckt.

Heute schreibe ich mit einer Perspektive
länger als die künstlichen Nägel,
die ich damals hatte. Ich erhasche eine Wiederholung
des Musikvideos auf YouTube,
bemerke zum ersten Mal,
dass diese Jungs,
wenn man sie auszieht und ihnen Glatzen rasiert,
abstürzen würden, heftig, wie Samson.
Und, Tawny?
Ich würde ihr beibringen Poesie zu schreiben –
nackt in Metaphern zu tanzen.

Aber bevor irgendwas
davon passieren kann,
werden meine Bremsen versagen
und ich werde
die Böschung runterkrachen
und zu Schrott fahren,
was von meiner Jugend übrig war.

Perspective

I don't know where I'm going.
But, I sure know where I've been.

En 1987, mon nouvel
hymne du style « Fuck you, world! »
est « Here I go again »
de Whitesnake,
que j'écoute en boucle
sur mon baladeur Sony
posé sur le siège passager
de ma Mercury Capri '76
à 400 dollars (payée en cash) –

En route vers
une série
d'accidents,
imprévisibles
et prévisibles,
je passe les vitesses,
fenêtres baissées,
et je roule le long
de la rivière Chattahoochee
derrière le lotissement
d'Eagle's Landing, m'imaginant
dans la peau de Tawny Kitaen
voltigeant
de Jaguar en Jaguar,
convaincue que le summum
du succès est d'avoir
une vedette de rock
à la chevelure
plus volumineuse que la mienne
me rouler
une pelle.

Aujourd'hui, j'écris avec une perspective
plus longue que les faux-ongles
dont j'avais l'habitude. Je tombe sur une reprise

de la vidéo sur YouTube,
notant pour la première fois,
que ces garçons-là
déshabillés,
et le crâne rasé,
tomberaient de haut, tel Samson.
Et, Tawny?
Je lui apprendrais à composer des vers –
à danser nue avec la métaphore.

Mais avant qu'une seule
de ces choses
ne puissent se passer,
mes freins vont lâcher
et je vais percuter
un talus,
envoyant à la casse ce qui reste
de ma jeunesse.

Sandra Danneil received her PhD in the American Studies at TU Dortmund University, Germany, where she currently works as a PostDoc and does research for her second book. In her dissertation project on *The Simpsons' Treehouse of Horror: A Cultural History of the Digital Age* she worked in the field of American cultural, television, and media studies. With a Master's degree in film- and television studies, Sandra Danneil has specialized in horror and gender studies, popular pessimism, and dystopian studies. Within this field, she teaches classes on film, representations of Blackness, video games, as well as auteurs like John Carpenter, Stephen King, and Margaret Atwood. Since 2020 she hosts the "Fear Academy" podcast on Spotify and an Instagram account of the same name to teach students in the production of creative content.

Randi Gunzenhaeuser is professor of American studies and the media at Dortmund University of Technology. She studied American literary and cultural studies as well as theater at Scripps College, California, and the University of Munich where she completed her PhD. In addition to articles on American literature, digital culture, theories of power, as well as urban studies, she published *Horror at Home: Genre,* Gender *und das* Gothic Sublime and her post-doctoral thesis (*Habilitationsschrift*) on machine people, *Automaten – Roboter – Cyborgs: Körperkonzepte im Wandel.* She taught American literary and cultural studies as well as media studies at University of Munich, Chemnitz University of Technology, and Siegen University.

Anne-Françoise Le Lostec is a lecturer of French and German in the School of Modern Languages at the Georgia Institute of Technology. An experienced language educator, her background includes the teaching of translation, essay writing, theatre, conversation, and German and French culture at Western Michigan University, the University of Northern Iowa, and the University of Regensburg, Germany. Her translation of Karen Head's poem "To the Roses of Auvillar" appeared in the 2014 issue of the *Atlanta Review*.

Karen J. Head, PhD, is the author of *Disrupt This!: MOOCs and the Promises of Technology* (a nonfiction book about issues in contemporary higher education), as well as five books of poetry (*Lost on Purpose, Sassing, My Paris Year, Shadow Boxes* and *On Occasion: Four Poets, One Year*). She also co-edited the poetry anthologies *Mother Mary Comes to Me: An Anthology of Popular Culture* and *Teaching as a Human Experience: An Anthology of Poetry*, and has exhibited several acclaimed digital poetry projects, including her project "Monumental" (part of Antony Gormley's *One and Other Project)* which was detailed in a *TIME* online mini-documentary. Her poetry appears in a number of national and international journals and anthologies. In 2010 she won the *Oxford International Women's Festival Poetry Prize*. She is editor of the international poetry journal *Atlanta Review*. On a more unusual note, she is currently the Poet Laureate of Waffle House – a title that reflects an outreach program to bring arts awareness to rural high schools in Georgia, which has been generously sponsored by the Waffle House Foundation. She was the inaugural Poet Laureate of Fulton County, Georgia. She is the Associate Provost for Faculty Affairs, and Professor of English and World Languages, at Augusta University. For twenty years, Head has been a visiting artist and scholar at the Institute for American Studies at Technische Universität Dortmund in Germany.

www.ingramcontent.com/pod-product-compliance
Lightning Source LLC
Chambersburg PA
CBHW030909170426
43193CB00009BA/793